DISCIPLESHIP
FOCUSED YOUTH MINISTRY

A Getting Started Guide for Parishes

Jim Beckman

&

Eric Gallagher

DISCIPLESHIPYM.COM

Contact: Discipleship Focused Youth Ministry;
eric@discipleshipym.com

ISBN-13: 978-1519671905
ISBN-10: 1519671903

Contents

Laying the Foundation

The Five Step Makeover Process

Closing Thoughts

1.
What is Youth Ministry?
Jim Beckman

"Remember: Christ is calling you; the Church needs you; the Pope believes in you and he expects great things of you!"
- Saint John Paul II - St. Louis 1999

I met Jonathan when he was a sophomore in high school. He showed up at the evening teen Mass one Sunday. I saw him from across the church and for some reason felt drawn to him. He looked sad to me, and dark. As we celebrated the liturgy, I found myself wondering what his story was. I made my way across to his side of the church immediately after communion, and thank goodness I did. As soon as he received communion, he went straight for the exit doors. I barely caught him as he was heading outside.

That first encounter was short – all I got was his name. But I remembered it. It was weeks before I saw him again, and like the previous time, I made an effort to get to him before he left, just to say, "Hi Jonathan, it's good to see you again." I could tell it made an impression. He even said something back to me about being shocked that I remembered his name. For the next several months, I had little conversations with Jonathan after Mass catching him before he left. But those casual conversations became more and more natural as time went on, and it almost seemed that he looked forward to me "finding" him. I would frequently invite him to stay for the youth group that was meeting after Mass, or at least to stay for dinner. "You have to eat, right?" I would reason with him. It was a long time before he accepted my invitation, but one night he did.

You could trace step-by-step Sherry Weddell's thresholds of conversion[1] through my relationship with Jonathan. It all started with that foundational question, "Can I trust you?" Unfortunately, it took more than remembering his name to secure that. But there came a time when I must have earned it, because he said yes to an invitation to more. Curiosity is the second threshold, and that is what brought Jonathan to dinner with me one night in the parish hall. It was a longer conversation than I had ever had with him and I was able to introduce him to a number of other teens at our parish. He still had that sad look about him, but there were actually a few smiles that night. Friendship and communication were yielding to openness. I learned that night where he went to school, what activities he was involved in, and a little about his family.

He didn't stay for youth group, but I pressed as he was leaving, "We should get together for lunch sometime." For the first time, I felt as if I had somehow crossed a boundary. I immediately felt a resistance from him, almost an uncomfortable shock that I would suggest something like that. I reeled back, trying to make it sound like it wasn't a big deal. I told him I knew that the school he went to had open lunch, and there were numerous places just across the street. I could just meet him there sometime. He could even invite some of his friends, my treat. I tried to play it all off nonchalantly, but I could tell something was wrong – he was not reacting well to the idea. It was an awkward parting. I thought I was being attentive to where he was at in the process, and trying to push a little, but not too far. Had I pressed too hard?

A couple weeks went by, and I didn't see Jonathan. He had started coming to Mass more consistently, and so when he didn't show up the

---

[1] Sherry Weddell, *Forming Intentional Disciples*, (Huntington, Our Sunday Visitor Publishing, 2012), chapters 5-8.

next Sunday, I was even more concerned that I had somehow pushed him away. But then one day I got a phone call – from his mom! When I realized who it was, I immediately thought the worst. I had all these fears running through my mind that she was calling to ask why I would ever invite her son to lunch. I remember the day well; I was driving when I got the call, and I literally had to exit the highway and pull over to talk with her. She made small talk briefly, explaining who she was and reminding me who her son was. Then she brought up the fact that I had invited him to lunch. "Here we go," I thought. But then she surprised me. "Are you going to do that soon?" she asked. "He hasn't stopped talking about it since you talked to him about it."

I was blown away – the complete opposite of what I was expecting. She went on to tell me what a rough time Jonathan had been going through, and how thrilled she was that I was pursuing him. "He really needs someone in his life right now, and his dad and I have been praying for something like this." Needless to say, I was calling him that night to set up a time to get together. To my surprise once again, when I offered him the option of bringing his friends, he said he would prefer to meet with me by himself.

That was the first of many lunches over the next year or so. And with each meeting, the conversation went a little deeper. We talked sports, movies, girlfriends, video games, etc. But eventually, we started talking about more significant things: dreams, things he wanted to do with his life, worldview, beliefs, etc. It was all very conversational, and whenever there was an opportunity to connect back to things happening at the parish, I would always invite him again to come join us. For a long time, he never responded to those invitations; he seemed more interested in the one-on-one conversations, which was fine with me.

I would periodically call Jonathan's mom. As I was getting to know him better, I wanted to stay connected to his family. I knew from experience how critical the connection with parents was, and at this point, Jonathan's family members weren't parishioners at our parish. She always seemed grateful for the connection and encouraging of the relationship. I could sense her deep concern for her son and a desire for him to awaken in his faith.

In time, Jonathan's openness led to seeking. He finally responded to one of my invitations – not to youth group, but ironically to a parish mission we were having. It was an older priest giving the mission, and I found myself regretting the invitation after the first five minutes of his talk. He was slightly boring and kept talking about science. Jonathan and his mom had come late, but I had saved them seats right in front of me. There I was, sitting right behind him. It was the first time he had actually come to something I invited him to, and I feared the worst. What if this priest didn't connect? What if this was a bad experience? Would I ever be able to get him to come to something else? I started praying like crazy. I literally was lifting my hand right behind his back, praying through the whole talk that God would somehow touch him, despite the dry presentation. I could see people disengaging all around me – I just kept praying harder.

At the end of the night, I was amazed when he said he really liked it. But he had lots of questions. The next several times we got together, it's all we talked about. Science, faith, reason, etc. I was continually surprised at Jonathan's intellect. The more I talked with him, the more I realized he was incredibly intelligent, and he had all these deep questions coursing through him. He just never talked with anyone about them. Once that door was opened, I couldn't stop him. It was like the lunch meetings weren't long enough. We were clearly into spiritual seeking now – lots of questions, lots of trying to get his head wrapped around what the church is and what we believe, and not quite sure it matched up with what he thought and believed. I'll never forget the day that he blurted out, "Who made all this shit up anyway!" He was referring to faith, and to the Catholic Church in particular. He had asked me a series of questions, and I was doing my best to navigate through answers. And that was his response. The whole thing seemed just a little too man-made to him – like a set of rules for a board game. It humored him.

I found myself not knowing how to react – I was cringing on the inside, almost expecting lightning bolts to come down from heaven. But I knew God was accepting Jonathan exactly where he was and had no demands or expectations on his response. His was a free invitation, and it was up to Jonathan how he would respond.

In time, Jonathan's spiritual seeking gave way to conversion. He eventually responded to an invitation to go to a Steubenville Youth Conference with our youth group. And it was a powerful conversion – life-altering, you could say. In the months after the conference, I couldn't believe the transformation. He decided that he needed to change schools because he had too many friends that were dragging him into his old lifestyle. Then he decided that he wanted to go to a Catholic high school so he could learn more about his faith. Then he started talking to me about wanting to be in a group that would help him grow. One of my first discipleship groups started with Jonathan.

As he matured spiritually over the next couple years, he felt the call to pursue priesthood and eventually entered the seminary. He has since discerned that God isn't calling him to be a priest, but the formation he got in the two years he was there has been monumental for him. It has been amazing to watch the transformation I have seen in this young man. What an incredible privilege it has been to "participate" in what God has been doing in his life.

I could go on for hours telling more of his story, but I think I've shared enough to make my point. The driving question of this chapter is, "What is youth ministry?" The answer, quite simply: what I did with Jonathan.

The whole time I was cultivating a relationship with Jonathan, I was still running our parish youth ministry. I was recruiting and training volunteers, planning weekly youth group nights, putting on retreats, organizing trips to the soup kitchen downtown, etc. It's not like my pursuit of him took up all my time. In fact, it was a very minor part of my time. Initially, I would only see him whenever he showed up at Mass. When I started meeting with him for lunch, it was periodic and was always dependent on <u>his</u> initiative. That's the beauty of a proper understanding of the thresholds of conversion. In the first several stages, you have to pursue the individual – until they feel like they can trust you, and they move into the thresholds of curiosity and openness. They will respond to invitations, but for the most part, it requires your pursuit. But once they enter the fourth stage of "seeking," they start pursuing you!

My main point, though, is to clarify that pursuing a relationship with Jonathan wasn't a full-time endeavor. I did it very off-to-the-side over 12-18 months. And I was actually pursuing several other teens in a similar way during that same time frame. I believe this is at the heart of youth ministry, whether you're a full-time paid youth minister, or a part-time unpaid volunteer. The context of youth ministry is relational – hands down. But the purpose of the relationship is to connect with a kid and walk with them through an encounter with Christ and into the early stages of discipleship until they get traction with the faith in their life.

Let's establish a working definition for youth ministry: all that is involved with helping teens embrace and mature in their faith in order to become authentic disciples of Jesus and fully engaged members of the Church. The defining document on Catholic youth ministry from the U.S. Bishops, *Renewing the Vision,* fully supports this definition. In the document, they identify three driving goals that set forth the aim of youth ministry:

- Goal 1: To empower young people to live as disciples of Jesus Christ in our world today.
- Goal 2: To draw young people into responsible participation in the life, mission, and work of the Catholic faith community.
- Goal 3: To foster the total personal and spiritual growth of each young person.

This definition helps us see what youth ministry should be—not necessarily what it currently is, but what it *should* be. And if we wanted to go one step further and provide a working definition of a "disciple," you could find a good one in the *General Directory for Catechesis*:

> The Christian faith is, above all, conversion to Jesus Christ, full and sincere adherence to his person and the decision to walk in his footsteps. Faith is a personal encounter with Jesus Christ making of oneself a disciple of him. This demands a permanent commitment to think like him, to judge like him and to live as he lived. In this way the believer unites himself to the community of disciples and appropriates the faith of the Church (GDC, 53).

This is the aim of youth ministry. It can seem daunting, perhaps, but it is our charge nonetheless. Your first reaction might be, "There's no way I could spend that much time with every kid." I would absolutely agree. Which is why you can't do youth ministry alone. You need lots of other adults and young adults who work together as a team. And, I would argue that there's no way to do it at all without a unique collaboration with their parents. It's not something we can fully accomplish on our own without their involvement. This is why I kept staying in contact with Jonathan's parents all through the process.

Youth ministry "involves" programs and retreats and meetings, and even things like ski trips and hiking and yes, maybe even pizza parties. It also involves education – teaching young people the content of our faith. But at the heart of what we are trying to do is to make disciples of the teens we are serving. That requires time, and an individual, personal approach. Each and every young person is going to have a different set of needs, unique challenges, and a very specific growth plan to help them get from where they are to where they need to be. Before we delve into discipleship, though, I think it is important for us to have a clear understanding of what conversion is. There is actually an identifiable path that most people go through on the journey to deeper faith. Let's call it the "process of conversion," or what the Church calls the Process of Evangelization. That will be the subject of the next chapter.

2.
What is Conversion?
Jim Beckman

"The sacred liturgy does not exhaust the entire activity of the Church it must be preceded by evangelization, faith, and conversion."
- CCC 1072

What we see exemplified/illustrated in Jonathan's story is "conversion." Earlier, I mentioned Sherry Weddell's thresholds of conversion. She lists five – trust, spiritual curiosity, spiritual openness, spiritual seeking, and conversion or intentional discipleship. But getting someone to a place of initial conversion, where they're ready to start becoming a disciple, is only the beginning of the process. There's much more that has to be done to help them mature in the faith. The Church calls this whole process "evangelization." I think it is helpful for our purposes to outline this progression in a bit more detail. To do that, I'd like to look at the overall process of evangelization the way the Church describes it (see diagram 2.1 on following page).

The Process of Evangelization

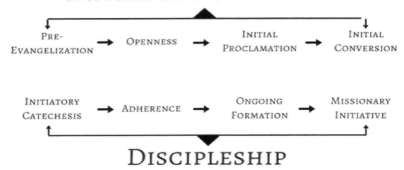

Diagram 2.1

For this diagram, and particularly the steps I have listed, I'm drawing from a number of magisterial documents, primarily the General Directory for Catechesis (GDC), but also Catechesi Tradendae and Evangelii Nuntiandi. In Evangelii Nuntiandi, Pope Paul VI first said that evangelization is a "complex process made up of varied elements." (EN, 24) In Catechesi Tradendae, John Paul II picks up on this theme and calls these varied elements "moments," going on to say that, "Catechesis is one of these moments - a very remarkable one - in the whole process of evangelization." (CT, 18)

We see a continued development of this thinking in the GDC, with numerous reference points for this diagram. If you read only Part I, chapters 1 and 2 on Catechesis, you would find most of these. (See specifically articles 47-49, 56-57, 61-62, 67-68 and 85-87). I am drawing from all of these sources to identify what's been laid out in this diagram – eight steps, or "essential moments" if you will, in the overall process of evangelization.

In the top tier (Pre-Evangelization, Initial Proclamation, Openness, and Initial Conversion), you could place all five of Sherry Weddell's thresholds from *Forming Intentional Disciples*. I'm just using a different scheme. Building trust and curiosity would fall into the phase of Pre-Evangelization in my model. Openness actually refers to the threshold of spiritual openness. Spiritual seeking would fall into Initial Proclamation and Sherry's conversion or intentional discipleship would be the same as Initial Conversion in my model. This gives us some vocabulary that we can use throughout the rest of the book. (see diagram 2.2 below)

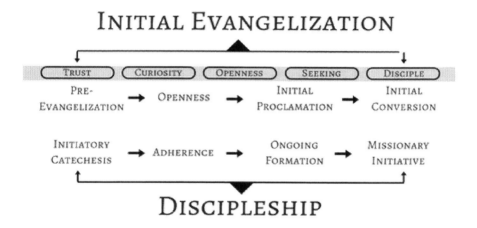

Diagram 2.2

The critical point is that the very important work of discipleship is often neglected in youth ministry. What we have seen in Catholic youth ministry in the past couple decades is a growing strength in the top tier of this process – what we could refer to as *Initial Evangelization*. We have more and more teens going to retreats, camps, conferences, and mission trips. They are hearing the Gospel message proclaimed, and many are opening up their hearts and are experiencing initial conversion. But what happens after initial conversion? In my experience, the activity on the bottom tier of this model is significantly lacking – the work of *intentional discipleship.* In fact, when it comes to teens who have experienced initial conversion, what many youth ministers do is jump them from their conversion to missionary initiative. This seems logical. A teen has a powerful conversion experience, so let's engage them in some role of peer leadership. But there is a major flaw in this thinking.

If we take a deeper look at the real meaning of leadership, we can see that there are two sides of the equation – what the leader does, but much more importantly, WHO the leader is as a person. If you look back to the diagram, jumping from initial conversion to peer ministry or service would be setting a teen up for failure by focusing on just the first part of the equation – what they do. You would be skipping the foundational steps of formation that help a young person to truly *become* a disciple.

This is the primary focus of this whole book and a particular emphasis of the next chapter. The steps in the overall process of evangelization that correlate with this activity of intentional discipleship are: Initiatory Catechesis, Adherence, Ongoing Formation, and Missionary Initiative. These are the critical stages of development that set up a young person to be an authentic disciple and follower of Christ. In the next chapter, I will develop a clear definition of discipleship and break down the principles that guide the method and practice of intentional discipleship ministry with teens.

3.
What is Discipleship?
Jim Beckman

"In virtue of their baptism, all the members of the People of God have
become missionary disciples"
- Pope Francis (EG, 120)

Once Jonathan had that initial conversion experience, my job wasn't done. In fact, it was just beginning. For him, the conversion happened at a Steubenville Youth Conference. I remember getting together with him several times during the rest of that summer. He was on fire! It was amazing to see the transformation that had taken place.

Jonathan had gone from this skeptical, disinterested teen who was caught up into all kinds of bad things to this "spiritual sponge," asking questions, trying to get a better understanding of what exactly we believe. He was at the critical stage in the whole process of evangelization called Initiatory Catechesis. This is where intentional discipleship has to be employed. If someone doesn't come and walk alongside a new convert and help them get traction in the early stages of discipleship, I find that people tend to stagnate. Some will even backslide from the faith and revert to their former ways.

This is why these stages are so important in the overall process. This is how you "seal the deal," and it's what makes the difference between a convert who becomes an authentic, lifelong disciple and a convert who never really gets any footing in their faith. They hang around, for a while at least. They get excited about church and are even faithful for a time. But when things get difficult, or a trial hits them, or friends start questioning their newfound faith – they waiver or can even fall away altogether.

I love how the GDC develops the stage of initiatory catechesis. It lists the fundamental characteristics of initiatory catechesis as: 1) comprehensive and systematic formation, 2) an apprenticeship of the entire Christian life, and 3) a basic and essential formation. (GDC, 67) Helping someone learn the content of our faith is a crucial part of forming them. There IS a content that needs to be imparted, and it should be done in a way that is systematic and comprehensive. It doesn't have to be ALL the content just yet, but rather the "basic" and "essential" stuff that gets right to the heart of what it means to follow Christ. And it needs to be imparted through an "apprenticing" model. That implies more than just transferring information. Apprenticeship is a powerful word. It's not just information, but "formation."

In addition to teaching the content of the faith, it is important that what is being taught is "adhered to." This is where I believe it is critical to adopt the method of mentoring. Adhering to the faith requires someone who models it, and this is what a mentor does. In its simplest articulation, you could say that mentoring is "teach, show, try, do." I teach someone a principle of our faith, I then show them how I apply it in my life, I then invite them to try to express it in their life. This may take several attempts with tweaking and direction. But eventually, they are free to go off and do it on their own.

Imagine if faith was taught this way across the board. Not just classes and talks with content, but individual, personal attention and intentional help assimilating what is being taught. I'm actually convinced that this is the missing ingredient in youth ministry today. In the past several decades, ministry offerings have become more and more programmatic. We've gotten away from relationships and intentionality. In the process, I think we've lost this aspect of modeling the faith and "walking with" someone into application. What would it look like if youth ministry was actually set up like this? What if the focus truly was making disciples?

To envision that, we have to have a definition for discipleship. We can return to our working definition of a disciple: someone with a "permanent commitment to think like him (Christ), to judge like him and to live as he lived . . . uniting oneself to the community of disciples and appropriating the faith of the Church." If that's the definition of a disciple, then "discipleship" would be all the work involved in helping someone become one of those.

The first thing you have to realize is that discipleship is not a one-size-fits-all enterprise. That would make it a "program," and that's exactly what we are trying to get away from. Discipleship is inherently individual and customized. I have learned over time that there are some common threads in discipleship – guiding principles, you could say. These are the core "traits" or the "secret sauce" that make it work. Along with understanding of the process of evangelization, the four earmarks of discipleship and the four areas of formation help articulate the vision of Discipleship Focused Youth Ministry. Let's start by looking at the four earmarks of discipleship.

The Four Earmarks of Discipleship

In order for our efforts to be fruitful, there are deep underlying principles to effective discipleship that need to be honored. Earmarks are what make something stand out from other things. I first heard these earmarks expressed by a popular author on discipleship, Greg Ogden. His book *Transforming Discipleship* has been one of my go-to text books for intentional discipleship.[2] These principles are what make Discipleship Focused Youth Ministry stand out from other traditional forms of youth ministry.

---

[2] Greg Ogden, *Transforming Discipleship*, (Downers Grove, Inter Varsity Press Books, 2007) pgs. 124-126.

Intimacy
Real discipleship requires depth and intimacy. As teens feel more and more safe, they will open up. You have to be aware that intimacy like this is not something most teens have experienced. It's somewhat foreign to them, and you have to help them navigate it in a healthy way.

Mutual responsibility
Discipleship is dialogical, meaning "two." There's a transference of knowledge, experience, and abilities that passes from the discipler to the disciple. But it also requires the participation, effort, and receptivity of the disciple. This is a two-way endeavor. In fact, the lion's share of the effort falls to the disciple, not the discipler.

Customization
Discipleship is unique to each and every person. It's not a one-size-fits-all proposition. It takes time to disciple, and the biggest share of that time is spent getting to know the individual person you are working with and working with them to create a customized growth plan that fits with their unique situation.

Accountability to life change
One of the things teens need is accountability. And for it to be effective, they have to first give permission to the person trying to hold them accountable. In our modern culture that is driven toward isolation and radical independence, teens will struggle with true accountability. They will need to be coached and mentored in it and shown healthy ways for it to be expressed in the context of your group.

The four earmarks of discipleship, in a way, are the "how" we cultivate an atmosphere for authentic discipleship. They are what you would be looking for in a relationship between the adult and the youth to measure whether or not what is happening, is in fact, discipleship. In other words, the four earmarks are the "how we teach".

The Four Areas of Formation

The four areas of formation on the other are the "what we teach". Traditionally in many areas of the world Catechesis has been limited to just the academic or intellectual approach. If a youth group exists in the parish, this approach will also often include a service component which gets into pastoral formation to some degree. The reason the four areas of formation are vital in Discipleship Focused Youth Ministry is because they offer insight into <u>total</u> formation. In many parishes, it is assumed that some formation is being done at home or in a Catholic school system. Discipleship Focused Youth Ministry seeks to recognize which areas of formation a youth needs to grow in and responds by offering opportunities for formation in those areas. It recognizes that if a youth needs to grow in ways beyond the knowing the teachings of the faith, that the parish should be supporting parents in those areas as well.

The four areas of formation have been excellently articulated by Saint Pope John Paul the Great in his Apostolic Exhortation *Pastores Dabo Vobis (On the Formation of Priests)*. This framework for formation was picked up by the U.S. Bishops as the lens through which they desire ALL lay faithful to be formed, but particularly those in roles of lay ecclesial ministry. Their document *Co-Workers in the Vineyard* describes this process in great detail. While I give a brief explanation of each below, it is recommended that you look into these two documents as well.

Spiritual Formation
Inviting teens into a deeper relationship with Jesus Christ through experientially learning about worship, prayer, and devotion. Rooting young people in a vibrant life of prayer is the best way to secure them as lifelong disciples.

Intellectual Formation
Helping teens learn about the Scriptures, the Catechism, and the Church in order to deepen the roots of their faith.

Human Formation

Empowering teens to create an authentic community of disciples and develop healthy relationships with their peers, their family, and their community.

Pastoral Formation

Encouraging teens to extend their development as disciples by putting their faith into action as they engage in contemporary cultural issues that they face on a daily basis in their lives.

These are the driving characteristics that help create a framework or structure for effective ministry. When you honor these principles, you develop a conducive environment where discipleship can actually happen. Foster the kind of environment in your small groups that reflect these characteristics, start building relationships with the teens, and you will be able to build from there.

I can honestly say that shifting to discipleship in ministry has been one of the most rewarding experiences in all my years of youth ministry. There is a tremendous power to the small group dynamic and the deep relationships that form over time. In the next chapter, Eric will share his hopes for youth ministry in response to the call of the New Evangelization and how Discipleship Focused Youth Ministry became the focus of his work.

4.
Forging New Paths
Eric Gallagher

"You either belong wholly to the world or wholly to God"
- St. Francis of Assisi

A few years ago, someone explained to me what a "desire path" was (see image on left). An example of a desire path would be a path through the woods that was not built, but was instead created by the foot traffic of many people who realized that it was a quicker or easier route to where they wanted to go. As a desire path gets used more and more frequently, it becomes clearer and easier to travel. There are actually some cultures in which they do not even build roads or sidewalks until they discover where and how people will navigate first. The idea is that they want to build where people need the sidewalks and roads the most. It may not be the easiest or quickest way to build a town, and the results may not be the most structured or attractive, but I am willing to bet it's a bit more productive and a better use of resources than it would have been otherwise.

In many ways, we have built up very structured systems in youth ministry, and it's these systems that guide our thinking and methods of doing things. When we become comfortable relying on these structures, the untraveled areas tend to look more scary, difficult, and messy. The longer these systems are used, the less willing we are to take a risk and create a desire path that makes is easier to get where we want to go. The Church understands this, which is why she is calling us to engage in a New Evangelization. The Lineamenta document written for the 2012 Synod on the New Evangelization describes it to be the "courage to forge new paths in responding to the changing circumstances and conditions facing the Church in her call to proclaim and live the Gospel today."[3] This is what Discipleship Focused Youth Ministry strives to do. Imagine starting youth ministry from scratch without any preconceived ideas of how things should be done and being able to create your own paths, giving you the best possible long-term results. Where would you start? What types of people would seek out to help? What type of job would you create for yourself? These are questions I have asked myself many times over 14 years of youth ministry.

The reason the first person begins to create a desire path is because they are willing to try new things or they realize that there is likely a better way to achieve the results they are looking for. Maybe they can even see the better route and are willing to take the first steps to creating a path that everyone can use. Several years ago, I made a list of things I desired in youth ministry but that I wasn't finding. Discipleship Focused Youth Ministry is a response to the seeking of these things. I still have this list and thought I would share it below:

A ministry that was healthy and balanced for all involved
I found youth ministry to be more and more difficult once I got married and started having children. I desired a youth ministry model that allowed for a more balanced lifestyle for myself and my family, as well

---

[3] Lineamenta on the New Evangelization for the Transmission of the Christian Faith, paragraph 5.

as all of the other volunteers and youth involved. I didn't want to have to "do" and be in charge of everything, but I wanted to inspire and lead others. I truly believed that being a youth minister with a growing family was something that was possible, but not using the model and methods I had known before.

A ministry that was scalable and reproducible

Every time I sensed growth in my youth group, I noticed great tension in how we were going to continue doing what we were doing. When we had a lot of fun and games, we would lose the youth that desired to go deeper (or just didn't like the games). When we would strive to go deeper, we would lose those who were not there yet. I desired a ministry model that met youth where they were at and that didn't require a dramatic alteration because of a shift in the number of those involved. However that was done, it needed to be reproducible, which likely meant it would need to be very simple in nature as well. Whatever "process" or "approach" worked, I wanted to be able to duplicate it in order to make it accessible to as many youth as possible.

A ministry that was parish-focused

When working with a youth group model, it seemed very disconnected from the family life of the youth and even separate from the parish community. Like everyone else, I would strive to integrate and bring these components into the youth ministry, but my desire was not to have to force things together. Rather, I wanted youth ministry to flow from and out towards the life of the family and the parish community, as well as the Catholic Schools.

A ministry that was customized based on the interest and needs of the youth

For many parishes, when a youth desires to be involved, they are asked two questions 1) what grade are you in? and 2) what gender are you? I desired a model that built on the needs of those involved instead of simply putting them with others because they were in the same grade. I desired that youth would be connected with others who would encourage them and hold them accountable in the ways in which they were being called to grow.

A ministry that targeted the youth through adults.
It took me awhile, but I finally discovered that my role was not to be the youth minister, but to train and form adults in the parish to be youth ministers. When that happened, I knew I desired a youth ministry model that was built on the understanding that it is not up to the youth minister to do everything, but to inspire the average Catholic in the parish to discover their charisms and use their gifts to bring others to know and love Christ.

These are some of the goals that I had set about five years into youth ministry. I knew that these were the things that I desired, but what I was doing in youth ministry was not creating these results. This is how Discipleship Focused Youth Ministry was born. It began by praying through tensions I was experiencing, but to which I truly believed God had answers.

5.
What is Discipleship Focused Youth Ministry?
Eric Gallagher

"Christianity without discipleship is always
Christianity without Christ."
- Dietrich Bonhoeffer

Taking in everything covered in the first four chapters can be very overwhelming, especially for someone who is just beginning in youth ministry. At the heart of Discipleship Focused Youth Ministry (DFYM) is a process that breaks all of these goals and components down into baby steps in order to create a process that is much more manageable. While DFYM does not guarantee immediate results, it does strive for a vision that is rooted in the teachings of the Church and aims for a depth that will bear fruit, as well as provide a more healthy and balanced approach.

Simply put, DFYM is a process that begins with discipleship as the starting point but also makes discipleship the goal for every aspect of youth ministry. Jesus spent His time forming disciples who were then given the task to go and make more disciples. The goal of Discipleship Focused Youth Ministry is the same, in that it seeks to form young people as disciples in a way that equips and inspires them to go and do the same with others. The goal is not just to form disciples, but to form people who can form people to be disciples.

Doing this on a parish level can be difficult because it requires someone who can form the disciple-makers (known as a Spiritual Multiplier). The vision and planning can start with just one small group, but in the context of a whole parish, a greater vision is needed. That is what we hope to dive into in this chapter: the process of executing a parish-wide vision for youth discipleship.

The process of getting started with DFYM in a parish can be broken down into five steps. Many times ministry is compared to planting seeds and growing fruit. You could look at these five steps the same way. This chapter will give an overview of those five steps, and we will dive into each one individually in the following chapters,

1. Take inventory (get tools & seeds, view landscape, etc.)
2. Cultivate an atmosphere for discipleship (till the soil and foster current growth)
3. Begin evangelization (plant seeds)
4. Adapt to growth and needs (prune, weed, plant more, etc.)
5. Feed the nations (give the abundance away)

What these steps do is to create a plan and a mindset in a parish that break down the process of evangelization to provide a more simplified and linear approach. When carried out correctly, the vision comes full circle, and all of the steps begin feeding into one another.

Discipleship Focused Youth Ministry is an approach to youth ministry that focuses on discipleship, relying on the power of discipleship to transform a few lives at a time, producing fruits in the lives of others that are then brought into discipleship, and the process goes on and on. Instead of trying to tackle everything all at once, this allows a parish to begin with one step at a time, gradually growing and building a solid program, and then eventually offering programs and initiatives that fulfill the mission "Ad Gentes" (meaning "To All Nations") all while remaining focused on discipleship as the goal and means to everything that they do.

6.
What is Needed to Get Started?
Jim Beckman

*"Being a disciple means being constantly ready to bring
the love of Jesus to others"*
- Pope Francis (EG, 127)

If you are still reading, hopefully that means that we have made a compelling case for Discipleship Focused Youth Ministry. This book, though, is only meant to lay a foundation. We've talked already in numerous places about how discipleship is unique, personal, specific, etc. It is going to look different at your parish than it does anywhere else.

You have to reject those thoughts you might be having about wanting a "cookie cutter" program that you can implement. I have heard lines like these: "It should be as simple as 'just add water and stir!'" Or, "It's as easy as putting in a DVD and hitting play!" Oh, if it only were that easy. I'm so sorry, but there is no silver bullet; there is no magic resource that will do all the work for you. And any resource or publisher that is promising you that is selling you a load of #!&*! Don't buy it. Be smarter than that!

I'm going to be honest with you from the very start. This is hard work. In fact, I believe it is one of the hardest things I have ever done in ministry. Getting into another person's life and earning the right to be heard; that in itself is a major accomplishment. But then you have to journey with them through the early stages of discipleship, and mentor them through the process. It's intimidating, humbling at times, and it stretches the heck out of you as a person. But I can tell you one thing, there is nothing more rewarding than helping someone get on the way as a disciple. When they take off and you see them getting traction and progress, it's amazing. But when you see them want to start discipling others and actually doing it, your heart just explodes. There's nothing like it, and it makes all the sacrifice worth it.

Before we turn to the practical application of discipleship, we need to talk about the "mindset shift" that has to happen. Before you launch out of the gate, I want to give you a number of basic pointers that will help guide the way.

Be a Disciple Yourself

You can't give what you don't have, and if you're not pursuing discipleship yourself, everything you do with a young person is going to come off lacking, or worse, inauthentic. Teens can spot a fake a mile away, and they will pull away from you if they sense hypocrisy. Every struggle that you go through yourself in pursuing holiness will inform and inspire what you are able to share with the young people you serve. Pursue it for yourself, and they will follow.

You also can't share with others what you haven't experienced yourself. If you have never BEEN discipled, it is going to be hard to disciple others. You have no context from which to understand it. I think this is one of our greatest poverties – most adults in the Church today have not experienced this being done for them. That was my experience as well. However, I have discovered that I've been able to find certain people who can disciple or mentor me in specific areas. I haven't been able to fill all the gaps completely, but what discipleship I have received has made a huge difference in what I am able to offer others. You need to pursue others who can disciple and mentor you in various aspects of the faith. It doesn't have to come all from one person; it can be a whole network of disciplers. Just pursue it!

Be Committed to Ongoing Training and Formation, First for Yourself AND for Your Leaders.
As I said earlier, I truly believe this is one of the greatest poverties in the Church today. We have an entire generation of adults who are poorly formed, and many who have been *mis*informed. It's like the pendulum swung from the Baltimore Catechism era to the "nothing" era. People rejected formation altogether and opted for more of a cultural or social connection to the faith that has left them with no foundation.

If you want to make an impact in the life of a young person, you need to KNOW the faith. At some point in the process, it's not going to be enough to just have your conversion experience to fall back on. You will need to help a young person embrace what we believe and live it out in their life. That can only happen if you are doing the same.

Let's take a moment to reflect on the same Four Areas of Formation in light of our need to be formed as adults in order that we might be more effective in forming others:

Spiritual Formation
Authentic discipleship invites us into a deeper relationship with Jesus Christ by experientially learning how to engage in relational prayer and practice spiritual disciplines. Being rooted in a vibrant life of prayer is the best way to secure lifelong disciples.

Intellectual Formation
We need to pursue knowledge of the Scriptures, the Catechism, Church history, and the foundational teachings of the Church in order to deepen the roots of our faith.

Human Formation
A critical aspect of discipleship is community. Coupled with the poverty of adult formation in the Church is the increased experience of individualism and isolation for many people. People are starving for relationship, and many don't even know it! They stay so saturated with

constant "noise" from the media that they are distracted from their true inner longings. True discipleship helps people connect, and helps them become increasingly self-aware in order to grow in deeper levels of intimacy and authentic community.

Pastoral Formation
The first three areas of formation extend their development as disciples put their faith into action – engaging in contemporary cultural issues that they encounter on a daily basis. Pastoral formation addresses the unique pastoral issues that each individual person faces in their own life, but also stretches them beyond themselves to be aware of the greater needs of the Church: evangelization, pastoral care for others, social justice, etc. In a nutshell, it is getting caught up in the apostolic mission of the Church. In pastoral formation, you learn how to give away what you have been given!

The bottom line in this area is to set a high bar. Get ready to be real and be honest. Be ruthless with yourself, and challenge yourself to greater and greater growth. The teens you lead will eventually become the kind of disciples that YOU and your leaders are. Be a step ahead of your leaders, and make sure your leaders are a step ahead of their teens: always learning, always growing, modeling the passion and dedication of lifelong disciples yourselves.

Be Creative – Get OUT of Your Box!
One of the biggest challenges I have seen is youth ministers or DRE's who are just locked in a mindset about what youth ministry is supposed to look like. You have to embrace that Discipleship Focused Youth Ministry is a complete makeover. You will have to defy the human resistance to change, not only in yourself but in all those around you.

And many who get past that obstacle get stuck trying to make discipleship into another "program." It all stems from a human condition we call control. We want to be in control and stay in control. Well, discipleship is *not* that. It's actually a decentralization of control. Instead of being a youth minister, you are making a bunch of other youth ministers – empowering many adults with the gifts, formation, and skills to be able to make disciples of young people themselves. Instead of you being in relationship with many teens - more than you can actually be effective with - you are empowering many adults to be in those relationships, but with a small group of teens so they can truly make an impact.

It's going to feel strange at first. You're going to feel like you are somehow giving up what you were trained to do. You're going to feel like you're losing connection with the teens. You may even struggle with a little jealousy – seeing other adults engage in relationships with teens who you are really drawn to. This is all very normal, and you have to avoid the human tendency to grasp at regaining control.

Finally, remember that discipleship is unique, and your Parish is unique. The way you shift to this approach is going to look different than any other parish. Don't have a set idea of what it is going to look like – rather let God lead you and the other adults working with you to a vision of what HE desires. And don't compare yourself or your ministry with other parishes – be yourself, and let the unique charisms of your parish community begin to enliven the ministry you are doing.

Work Smart, Not Hard

Instead of trying to force a discipleship approach, it is sometimes more prudent to look for areas of momentum that already exist. In one parish, the pastor himself was the primary lead. He kept trying to get adults to start discipleship groups and was getting frustrated with the lack of results. Then one day, he realized that he had 6-8 young men serving as altar servers who seemed to always be hanging around the sacristy during Mass times. He saw a natural momentum in the server group. So he just started a discipleship group with them and a couple of other adults. The teens were very receptive, and he was able to train and equip the adults by modeling for them how he was leading the initial group. Over time, word spread about this group, and other teens started asking if they could be involved. It was a very organic development to let the couple of adults start new small groups, and by that time other adults had emerged who were also interested in leading.

Survey the landscape of your parish. What are the unique charisms and passions in your community? What types of activities and ministries already exist? Can you identify areas of natural momentum, where people are already engaged and responding? It's always easier to hinge on these successes as you are getting started. It will help you get traction more quickly.

In another parish, they were trying to start discipleship groups with the older teens who were sophomores and above. They had spent the past year going through several cycles of unsuccessful attempts. As we talked about what all they were doing, I discovered that they had a summer camp for 8th graders that was hugely successful. They estimated that 85-90% of the 8th graders attended this camp during the summer between 8th grade and high school. In their own words, they told me that the teens came back from this experience "on fire." When I asked what happened to all those teens after camp, I found out that they were moved into a year-long Confirmation preparation that was facilitated by one of the teachers at the local Catholic high school. It was a classroom model, not very engaging, and by the time it was over in the spring, attendance had typically dwindled to next to nothing. The teens were confirmed late in the spring and then had nothing really going on during the summer. It was during their sophomore year that they were invited to join the youth group.

Can you see the gaping hole here? You have traction and momentum with a bunch of 8th graders coming off of a powerful summer camp experience, and then they are shoved through a mediocre, boring classroom-model Confirmation program that allows them over a year to completely disengage. Then you try to reconnect with them as sophomores; it's NOT going to happen. I simply suggested, why not start the discipleship groups as they are going through Confirmation?

You could get the leaders to participate in the summer camp experience to begin the relationship building process. The leaders could then go right into their freshman year and use the discipleship groups to walk the teens through Confirmation prep. This would require a revamp of the Confirmation program, but there are several great resources out there now that lend themselves to a small group dynamic. Then, at the end of the year when they all get confirmed, you just invite the teens to continue meeting together as a discipleship group. It's natural and organic, and not nearly as hard as trying to re-engage teens who have been virtually disconnected for over a year. The biggest challenge to this would be getting enough adults leaders to keep the whole thing going from year-to-year. You are literally going to need new adults every year, because my guess is that the vast majority of those teens will desire to stay in their small groups.

Those are just a couple of examples, but you get the idea. Work smart, not hard! Also when you survey the landscape, look for areas of wasted energy. Are there ways you are putting a lot of energy into things that aren't really bearing any fruit? Don't be afraid to ask the tough question: why are we doing this? "Because we always have" is not an adequate answer. Don't be afraid to cut the chaff, but slowly and carefully. Remember, people are always resistant to change. Don't cut too many things at the same time.

And most importantly, let God do the "heavy lifting." Pray, pray, pray. In the words of St. Augustine, "Pray as if everything depended on God, and work as if everything depended on you."

Have the Right Disposition
You've heard the old adage, "You catch more flies with honey than with vinegar." Well, it's true! Don't be a bulldozer! You have to be keenly aware that change is just hard for people. It's not so much that people resist change as much as they resist losing what they are comfortable with or have found fruit in before. If you push too hard or try to go too fast, they will resist it with every fiber of their being. The shift to a

discipleship approach doesn't have to happen overnight, and it doesn't need to be a daunting overhaul of everything you are doing. I'm actually not a big advocate of "blowing things up" to make the change. I find that many who have approached it that way have created more problems for themselves than it was worth. They were just trying to change too fast.

I'll say it again: people are naturally resistant to change. So when you make huge changes all at once, you are going to get a ton of pushback – from teens, from parents, from other staff . . . maybe even from your Pastor. I'm more a fan of what I would call "dual tracking." Keep the existing things you are doing going, but more in a maintenance mode. Start the discipleship efforts off to the side, but start small, just one or two groups at a time. This gives you plenty of time to recruit and train leaders and allows the discipleship shift to happen more organically. And most importantly, without all the political fallout that can happen when you try to push it too fast. I've found that in most of the places that have approached it like this, they have seen the shift happen in less than two years, sometimes even faster.

And when you are making changes, many times you can make little cuts when groups of teens are moving on or graduating, as well as starting new things with new incoming classes. This creates the least amount of resistance. The new incoming classes won't even recognize that you made a change because they aren't already acclimated to the "way things are." Let the results and fruit speak for itself. It's hard to argue with fruit and results. Over time, you will move mountains – you just have to be patient.

Tenacity! A Key Characteristic of the New Evangelization
And for the last point, I want to encourage the character quality of tenacity. Don't give up, don't give in, don't accept NO for an answer! If you're turned down for one idea, go back with another. Remember that the stories of countless saints throughout our history are filled with these kinds of situations. They were convicted by what God was calling them to do, and there was NO STOPPING them.

You and I need to be like that. Maybe someday people will look back on this era of history and be amazed at the few people who ushered the shift to discipleship into the Church. Wouldn't we be blessed to be counted among that group? It's going to be a tough go, and I'm afraid at times lonely. People will disagree with what we're trying to do; we'll get criticized and challenged and may even lose our job. Keep going, stay committed to the bigger vision – the Church desperately needs this kind of approach. People will resist, they will complain that this is not "how we do things." You have to push through. Be compassionate, and take your time with people. Help them adjust to the changes that need to be made by helping them see the fruit of what you are asking them to do.

I call this "tenacity." It's defined as the "quality or fact of being very determined; determination." Check out the synonyms: persistence, perseverance, doggedness, strength of purpose, tirelessness, indefatigability, resoluteness, resolve, staunchness, steadfastness, staying power. Would you consider yourself tenacious? Tireless, dogged, resolved in your pursuit of what the Lord is calling you to do? That's the spirit you need to have for this work. Pray that the Lord would help you have it, burning deeply in your heart, and that He himself would inspire it within you.

But the key question is, how? How do you get started in this new direction? In the next chapter, I will dive deep into the steps to get things started.

7.
Step 1 - Take Inventory
Jim Beckman

"If you are willing, my son, you will be taught, and if you apply yourself you will become clever. If you love to listen you will gain knowledge, and if you incline your ear you will become wise. Stand in the assembly of the elders. Who is wise? Cling to him. Be ready to listen to every narrative, and do not let wise proverbs escape you. If you see an intelligent man, visit him early; let your foot wear out his doorstep."
- Sirach 6:32-36

The first step you should take is to inventory what you have. Take a good look at your parish and assess the landscape. What areas of traction are already there for intentional discipleship? Are there individuals who are already committed disciples? Is there anyone else who could join you in this endeavor? Here are some key areas to which you need to pay attention:

Pastor and parish staff
Is there an openness and support for a shift in approach? You need to identify the people who might be entrenched in an old system who would directly oppose you. If one of those people is the pastor, you need to focus energies first on him and sell him on a new vision before moving forward. If the pastor is on board already, you need to make sure that none of the key opposers would have the pastor's ear and be undermining your efforts at every turn.

Be clear and up front that this approach is an investment model and is therefore slower. Be sure you don't set up an expectation for big numbers, fast growth, etc. It will be just the opposite. The first year will be slow growth as you identify and train key adult leaders and begin the process. The growth will happen faster in the second year, but it will still seem slow compared to a large group model. But in the third year, you will start to see the shift. Authentic discipleship always wins out in the long haul. Get your pastor and other key staff to focus on the long-term, and keep reminding them that this is what you are building for.

Budget and resources
Are there any budget resources that can be earmarked for intentional discipleship and for training of adult leaders? Can you advocate for such resources, and each year as you grow ask for more?

Your primary needs will be for training resources, bringing in speakers/trainers, development and mentoring of adult leaders and parents, and possibly for discipleship group content resources once you start meeting with teens.

Facilities
Most parishes have been designed with large group ministry in mind. There's one large meeting space for all teens, and you are discouraged from using any other spaces for fear of retribution from some other staff members.

What is the landscape of your parish in regards to meeting spaces? If you had multiple small groups meeting, is there adequate space at the parish to accommodate many small groups in smaller spaces all around the parish rather than in one large group space?

What are the policies in your diocese? Are small groups allowed to meet in host homes? If so, what are the protocol and guidelines for such meetings? Will your pastor support small groups meeting in homes? (I have seen some parishes where the diocese allows it, but the pastor won't, so you need to be sure). I have found that the home environment is actually the best way to foster the kind of dynamic we are striving for in these discipleship groups, but you need to remain in compliance with the Child Protection policies in your home diocese, and that may not be possible for you.

Diocesan Office for support and vision
While you are checking with your diocesan office about policies for safe environment, find out if there is any support for a discipleship approach. You would be surprised how many dioceses are moving in this direction, and you may find some critical support for your efforts. It may not be coming from the Youth Ministry Office, though that is where you should start. But also see if your diocese has an Office for Evangelization, or an Office for the New Evangelization. You may find some great support from those offices as well. Get on mailing lists/e-Newsletter lists from these offices so you can be informed of what they are doing: training opportunities, resources, vision from the diocese or the bishop, etc.

Community and support in the area
Are there other parents or adults in your parish that hunger for this type of ministry to happen for their children? Are there other parishes in your area that have shifted to intentional discipleship? Start praying for the Lord to make these connections for you, to bring about awareness of any resource or person in your area that might be a support for what you are doing.

Recruit some other adults to begin joining you in this prayer - find the people who are praying every day, going to Mass every day, praying in the adoration chapel frequently, etc. Get them lifting you and this new approach to ministry up in their prayers, and specifically praying that Jesus would be true to His promise, "Beg the Harvest Master to send laborers for His harvest." Jesus wouldn't direct us to say that prayer if it wasn't going to be answered!

Thriving or dying ministries in the parish

Part of your inventory should be to identify any thriving ministries in your parish overall, especially for adults. Are there any thriving, growing ministries going on at your parish? Are you seeing conversions happen in any of these? Many of these types of ministries spring up, but because there is no real mission connected on the other end of conversion, they lose steam and dwindle over time. All conversion is meant to be followed by formation and mission. The discipleship efforts that you have a heart for may be the exact thing a thriving ministry needs to continue growing! But you also want to get connected to the leaders of any thriving/growing ministry in your parish. They have already navigated the path that you are on, and they can be an immense help to you.

It's also good to become aware of the dying ministries in the parish. Are there ministries or organizations that have dwindled and are focusing more and more on "maintenance" rather than "mission"?

Adults who fit the bill to begin discipleship or maybe that you want to start investing in

There is a poverty of adult disciples in the Church. But that sometimes makes it easier to identify them - they stand out. Authentic disciples stand out in the typical parish through the way they pray and engage in the life of the parish. You need to start looking for those kind of people. Begin praying for them. Over the years, one of my most effective volunteer recruitment strategies has simply been a Novena to the Holy Spirit. I wouldn't even start the novena until I had info packets, and space in my calendar to respond, because once I started praying, people would just come out of the woodwork and ask how they could get involved. I had to be ready to handle the influx.

You don't need a ton of volunteers to get started, though. In fact, it's better to start small, with a small number of adults that you can truly mentor and work with to train. We will go over this in more detail in the upcoming chapters, but the idea is to start one or two groups at a time, and build from there. It's not uncommon to feel like you have very little to get started. Fortunately, you don't need much. Having too many adults and too many small groups simultaneously can actually complicate things and make it more difficult anyway.

8.
Step 2 - Cultivate an Atmosphere for Discipleship
Jim Beckman

"Faith in Christ and discipleship are strictly interconnected."
- Pope Benedict XVI

After taking inventory, you need to start building an atmosphere for discipleship. There is a fertile ground for discipleship, just like in a garden. If you wanted to plant a garden, you would never just go out and start planting seeds in your backyard. You would first have to clear the ground, dig up weeds, get rid of the grass, etc. Starting the process of discipleship is very similar. You have to prep the soil.

Throughout this book, we have been talking about all the right "ingredients" that help foster authentic discipleship. In this chapter, we want to resurface all those things in one place to show what the "fertile soil" for discipleship looks like. Here are the critical things that make for an atmosphere that fosters discipleship and true spiritual growth: the key "ingredients" of discipleship, the "activities" of the Church, the earmarks of a discipleship approach, and the four areas of formation. You can see these things as the tangible ways you can prepare the soil so that when you start your first discipleship group, it will actually begin to thrive because you are planting it in fertile soil, and the whole environment around it is fostering spiritual growth.

Creating this kind of environment is the role of the "spiritual multiplier." This is what you want to begin seeing yourself as. You are the one who is creating an atmosphere where those who desire to grow in their faith can actually do so. Authentic discipleship is not just serving in a leadership role or doing some service outreach, particularly when you haven't even been adequately prepared for it. I can't tell you how many youth ministers I have met over the years who told me that their "discipleship" program is getting their older teens to serve as peer leaders in their program. This is NOT discipleship. It might be a way to launch young people into missionary initiative, but if they haven't been prepared and truly formed for a leadership role, it is very likely that they will fail in the effort, and sometimes the elevation can do more harm than good.

Always remember: being a spiritual multiplier means not only feeding and directing those who are being discipled, but in making an investment in their personal lives. Much of discipleship is about relationship and mentoring, which just takes time. You have to carve out that kind of time in your schedule and be willing to take the time when it is needed.

The Key "Ingredients" of Discipleship
Discipleship primarily converges around three critical activities: Relationship, Content, and Mentoring. You can't disciple someone if you're not in relationship with them, and an intimate one at that. There is a content to discipleship, everything from the content of the faith to learning how to grow in true Christian friendship. However, a critical activity that is often overlooked is mentoring. Authentic discipleship involves mentoring, or even "apprenticing" someone in the application of the content. Think of a physical trainer. What does a trainer do for someone who is desiring to get into physical shape? They show them the right exercises, demonstrate how to do them the right way, and hold them accountable to doing those exercises consistently. The only difference with discipleship is that the "content" is all about growing in deeper relationship with Christ and patterning your life after His.

The "Activities" of the Church

If we had to narrow the activities of the Church down to a short list, we can find a great articulation for it in Acts 2:42: "And they devoted themselves to the apostles' teaching and fellowship, to the breaking of bread and the prayers." And just a verse or two later, we hear how the Lord added to their number every day. I capture these "activities" as: shared prayer, shared fellowship, shared learning, shared mission. We can see how these are the key things we are doing every Sunday when we gather together to celebrate the Liturgy. It's what makes us Catholic, and all these years later we are still doing the same things the people in the early Church started with.

Well, if those are the key activities of the larger Church, then every smaller extension of the Church should be a sort of microcosm of those activities...every small faith-sharing group, Bible study group, RCIA group, discipleship group, etc. You can even point to the family, which has been defined as the "domestic church," and see these are the key activities that should be done consistently and intentionally as a family unit. When we share in prayer, share in fellowship, share in learning, and share in mission, it has a tendency to connect us to the larger organism that we are meant to be a part of: the larger Church.

Think of it like a four-legged stool. The four legs are the "activities": shared prayer, shared fellowship, shared learning, shared mission. The seat of the stool is the small group. The legs are meant to support the seat and give it stability. We all know that a stool can't stand on one or even two legs. So if you start a small group to do service projects, and that's all that you do, the "stool" is not going to last long. I have seen this over and over again through the years. Groups that form around one focus like that just don't last. Even groups that have two of the legs won't sustain. They will last a little longer, but eventually will tip over.

Where you really start to see traction in small group settings is when you get the focus around several of these activities simultaneously. A three-legged stool will stand; a four-legged stool is even more stable. This is part of helping set up small groups for success: have them very intentionally include all four activities in the normal rhythm of their meetings. You don't have to do all four activities every time you meet, but over the course of any semester, you should see a consistent rhythm of all four: shared prayer, shared fellowship, shared learning, shared mission. Shared prayer and shared fellowship are easier to layer on top of each other in the same meeting, and shared learning becomes a part of our content pursuit on a regular basis. I typically include one or two "mission" activities per semester.

The Earmarks of a Discipleship Approach

We talked about these back in chapter three: intimacy, mutual responsibility, customization and accountability to life change. These critical earmarks, or characteristics of discipleship, need to be honored. As you build your ministry, you have to stay true to them and make sure that what you are building, particularly as it grows, consistently reflects them.

I am convinced that, as I said in chapter three, you can't stay true to these principles without using a small group or mentorship model. Large groups inherently defy all four earmarks.

The Four Areas of Formation

Again, we discussed these in chapter three: human, spiritual, intellectual, and pastoral. I like to think of them as "Gifts Received" for human, spiritual, and intellectual, and "Gifts Given" for pastoral. The whole discipleship process is all about patterning one's life after Christ by growing in deeper relationship with Him, and then sharing the gift of that new life with others. Human, spiritual and intellectual formation are all about the patterning of one's life; pastoral formation is all about how to share it and give it away to others.

These are the critical things that help make up the environment, or atmosphere, if you will, for fostering authentic discipleship and spiritual growth. The last thing I want to emphasize is the human aspect to all of this. Your tendency is going to be to look for a "program" to help you do all this. And as we have said before, there are many programs or resources out there that will promise to do all this for you. After having been involved with youth ministry for 30 years and doing intentional discipleship, in my personal opinion, such a program doesn't exist. Not only have I never seen one, but I don't even think it is actually possible to create one. In the same way that you can't really do effective discipleship within a solely large group setting, there's no one resource or program that could effectively meet the needs of every parish and every teen.

Have you ever seen the Saturday Night Live skit with Will Ferrell and David Alan Grier, *Wake Up and Smile?* It's the 20th anniversary of the morning show *Wake Up and Smile*. During the broadcast, they suffer a breakdown of the teleprompter. "What are they going to do with no words! No one is telling them what to say!" The show unravels quickly and breaks down into a Lord of the Flies-esque scenario. If you've never seen it, it's worth checking out; it's so stupid, it's hysterical.

The skit makes me imagine what things might be like in the Church today if you took away all the resources. What if the publishers all went away, and we actually had to do our ministry with nothing but the Bible, the Catechism and our own know-how? Or maybe the government made them all illegal! I think people would FREAK OUT! Just like in the skit, people would freeze up and panic. "There's no resources for my Confirmation class!! What am I going to do?! I don't know how to make a real disciple without a resource!! You mean there's no DVD, no VIDEO lesson?! I have to TEACH this myself?! What am I going to do?!!"

You get the idea - the whole thing would unravel quickly. I'm not saying resources and DVDs/video teachings are bad. I was one of the founders of YDisciple, so I am actually a fan. I just think it's unfortunate how dependent we have become on them. Some people can't figure out what they would even do it without one.

That is a far cry from what we are advocating, and it's the reason why we keep saying over and over again that this is not about a "program", nor is it some kind of "silver bullet." Real discipleship takes effort, and it requires you to know what you are doing to help someone navigate the growth process of following Christ. And you can only do that if you have done it yourself.

Now that doesn't necessarily mean that you have to have been "discipled" yourself. There are many, many adults today who never experienced being discipled. They never had someone mentor them in the faith and through the growth process involved. I actually see this as one of the greatest poverties in the Church today. We just don't have many strong adult disciples. But don't despair. I believe it is possible for one to make up the gap in their own personal experience and become an excellent disciple-maker, even if they never were discipled themselves.

Discipleship in its very essence is more about directing or guiding passion and desire than taking on the heavy lifting of the growth itself. That is the burden of the disciple, not the disciple-maker. This is what I was talking about back in chapter three, with the four earmarks of a discipleship approach. The earmark of "mutual responsibility" is critical. You can't disciple someone who doesn't desire growth and is willing to put in the effort to pursue that growth. Again, think of it like a personal trainer. If you went to the gym and started a new workout regimen, you might consider accessing a personal trainer to help you. The trainer can't do the workout for you; they can't lift the weights, or even show up at the gym for you. That burden is all on you. What the trainer will help with is pointing you in the right direction to get the biggest impact for your efforts.

This is what discipleship is like. And because it is, there's still hope if you were never formally discipled by someone else. If you desire growth and are willing to put in the effort to pursue that growth, you can understand the discipleship process and have most likely navigated it for yourself over time. You maybe have even accessed others who served as "disciplers" without them even knowing that's what they were doing. Perhaps it was limited to a specific area or need in your life, but you had someone help you in the growth process. Over the course of my life, I have had older, wiser people help me with everything from spiritual growth to managing my finances. It was usually for a limited time and specifically around a certain need, but in reality, that was a form of discipleship. They were helping me to grow in some area, and they guided my own desire for that growth so I could get the greatest impact for my efforts.

9.
Step 2b - Start the First Group(s)
Eric Gallagher

"To love God is something greater than to know Him"
- St. Thomas Aquinas

Starting the first discipleship groups is a crucial, practical part of cultivating an atmosphere for discipleship (step 2). Note that "cultivating an atmosphere for discipleship" comes before "begin evangelization" in the list of "baby steps." There are two important reasons for this. First, having a concrete, customized opportunity ready to go for the youth when they come back home from a conference or camp will give them greater confidence in saying "yes" to the way of discipleship laid out for them at the event. Second, it provides a way to begin investing immediately in the youth who are ready for it.

I am willing to bet that most, if not all, of the programs that are currently going on in your parish are helping the young people grow in their faith as disciples of Christ. While they may be helpful, I advocate a discipleship model because the amount of impact I have seen from it sets it apart from any other approach to youth ministry I have encountered before. Cultivating an atmosphere for discipleship is creating a place where all four of the earmarks of discipleship (intimacy, mutual responsibility, customization and accountability to life change) are present. Most often, this is done through a mentorship relationship between an adult and a youth or through a small group setting. We will focus primarily on small groups in this chapter because they are the most common method used to establish a norm of discipleship in a parish.

Getting the first small group(s) started can be a little tricky, especially if you already have an active youth ministry in your parish. No matter the size of the parish or the initial interest in discipleship, I recommend starting with only 1-3 groups. This helps ensure you can lay a good foundation, learn the ropes, and set some standards that will help new groups start in the future. It is extremely important to start discipleship groups in a way that communicates how a discipleship group is different. The depth and commitment of a discipleship group can be extremely attractive to youth who are ready to take the next step. When it is clear that a discipleship group is truly helping and engaging youth where they are at, the growth of discipleship in a parish will happen very naturally and organically.

For the sake of clarity, here is the process of starting and growing a group in six simple steps:

1. Discern and Ask the Right Adults
Discipleship is about following after a teacher as an apprentice. In order for this to work, it is vital that you start with someone who you believe can teach the traits of being a disciple well. This is someone who is not only a disciple themselves, but has the desire and the call to share that experience with others. You are looking for adults who pray, are devoted to the Sacraments, are patient and understanding with others, and will be learners. You want to identify those adults who are aware of how God is acting in their lives and who desire to teach others to discern what God is doing in their lives as well. They need not have had any youth ministry experience before. A great place to start is with some of the parents in the parish who are clearly already leading their own children deeper in the faith.

2. Train/Form the Adults

The next step is to train your adults to understand the vision and the purpose of discipleship. In the simplest formula:

The role of a Discipleship Leader is to observe young people using the four areas of formation as a guide and craft a plan for their formation

A Discipleship Leader does this by cultivating an environment where the four earmarks of discipleship (intimacy, mutual responsibility, customization and accountability to life change) exist.

The best way to really begin building a team and helping the adults involved in your ministry grow into their discipleship roles is to also teach and form them through discipleship (once again, using the four earmarks). If you can create an atmosphere of discipleship in which your adults can grow as disciple-makers, Discipleship Focused Youth Ministry will really begin to gain momentum. But training your adults must be more than simply giving them the game plan and telling them to "go!"; it's about walking with them and forming them individually as disciple-makers.

Typically, it is helpful to begin this training and formation time with an initial boot camp that goes through the basics of a discipleship approach (see DiscipleshipTraining.com). If other discipleship groups already exist in a parish, you may want to incorporate a period of apprenticeship or "on the job training," during which new leaders can sit in and learn the ropes from others. In many parishes, this involves a monthly gathering of adults focused on helping them grow in their understanding of the mission of discipleship. It is not so much training as it is being in community with others, learning from one another, and receiving through that community. It's taking the time to pray, check-in, and "reset the compass" ensuring that you are on the right track in your efforts of discipleship.

3. Invite the Young People

Once the adults have a good idea of what their role is and you sense that they are ready, send them out to begin inviting and getting to know their youth. The more naturally these adults can connect with the youth they will be discipling, the better the results will be. Maybe the adults already know and have some relationships with youth in the parish. If not, try to have them get to know one another in the context of other opportunities and events. You only need 2 or 3 youth to get going and to start meeting regularly. But once again, I cannot stress enough the importance of it being a natural process.

4. Strive for the Four Earmarks

The next step is to begin doing what you can to establish a good foundation for discipleship. This is where the four earmarks come in. The earmarks act as fertile soil so that the seeds you plant in your regular meetings can settle in. The more trust and sense of belonging you establish in your group, the greater the results you will see. Do not be afraid to take things slowly and simply enjoy spending time together. If you are starting with a group of youth who are not yet ready to dive into the challenges and commitments of daily prayer and missionary activity, take even more time. If your group is starting because a few youth went to a large conference or a retreat and came home ready to run, you can take things a little faster. Look to the story that Jim shared at the beginning as a model of relationship and slowly inviting to go deeper over time.

5. Make Commitments

After some time, every group will begin to settle. Some youth may not desire to be involved anymore; some new youth may have joined. Once you are at a point where youth are clearly committed to the group and are able to start opening up to each other more and more, it is time to take it to the next level. In a group that began with a lot of social, bonding activities, it is the leader's job to bring the youth through the process of clearly defining the group's purpose and agreeing to hold one another accountable to certain commitments or goals. It is very important not to assume that the purpose of the group was fully understood or grasped by every group member from the beginning.

Many times, it is helpful to have everyone in the group sign a group covenant. This covenant could include a commitment to the weekly meetings, being actively involved in the parish, commitment to daily prayer and regular reception of the Sacraments, commitment to an active missionary life, etc. The goal is that every member would understand that they are committed to the group because it exists to help them grow as a disciple of Christ and the members of the group are there to hold each other accountable to that growth.

6. Grow

I remember buying a $1 seed pot for my son one day that came with a small plastic pot, soil, and a small packet of seeds. It was a dummy-proof way to show him how to plant something and watch it grow. Similarly, when you have all of the fundamental aspects of discipleship in place, it is difficult for it NOT to grow. Once you have led your group to a point where they are urging one another on in their faith and experiencing the fruit of discipleship, the group will begin to grow, and you, like any gardener, will have to discern what to do with that growth.

The one thing I must caution at this point is that the focus should be primarily on vertical growth, meaning a focus on the depth of those with whom you are working. Do not be so concerned, especially in the beginning, about growing horizontally (with getting more groups started or more people involved in the parish). What I have found over and over again is that the others will come. If Discipleship Focused Youth Ministry is feeding the adults involved in your ministry, they will invite more adults to come. If the youth are being changed as a result of this ministry, their parents will be more engaged, and more youth will come.

10.
Step 3 - Begin Evangelization
Eric Gallagher

"To the Christian there is no such thing as a "stranger", there is only the neighbor...the person near us and needing us."
- St. Edith Stein

When I first started talking with priests in our diocese about different events and opportunities being offered, I was struck by one who told me that he didn't send any youth to these activities because he didn't have anything to offer them at the parish when they returned home. At first I was taken aback by his comment, but I later realized some of the truth and wisdom in his thinking. This is exactly the reason we must first cultivate an atmosphere for discipleship. When youth have an encounter with Jesus Christ that moves them towards a conversion in their life, you want there to be a place in your parish for those seeds of faith to be able to grow.

The small group structure described above can be replicated and grown on any scale. If one small group grows to be too big, it can be split. (More will be said about how to do this in Chapter 11.) If you need more small groups, you simply repeat the process above.

Once you have created a space where there is fertile soil, it is time to begin planting seeds. Be sure to leverage whatever parish-wide efforts or initiatives you might already have that draw young people to desire a to commitment to discipleship. Referring back to the process of evangelization described in chapter two, it is now time to focus on those youth who are not yet in the discipleship phase of the process.

To give you a better idea of how to "begin evangelization," here are six simple tips to get your gears moving in the right direction.

1. Use the fruit of discipleship to plant more seeds
One of the most effective ways to reach those who are not already involved is by using the fruits borne through your existing discipleship groups. Rather than going out after each individual person, invest in the disciples in the parish, and equip and encourage them to go and make more disciples among their peers and others to whom they are connected in the parish. If a discipleship leader is fostering evangelization (which is one aspect of pastoral formation) with the youth they are mentoring, there will be a natural overflow of what is happening in their own lives into the lives of those around them. The fruits of their own growth will be shared with others. This can take time, but when it begins to happen, it takes shape in profound ways that only God could have inspired.

2. Create a marketing plan for those NOT in discipleship
Make a list of all of those NOT currently in discipleship. Create a plan to reach and get them connected with other youth and adults in the parish. Take time to look at the demographics of those not involved in a group, and work with others to determine what it will take to get them there.

The goal of this is not simply to get everyone involved or to create more work, but to become more aware of opportunities to send those whom you are investing in to impact specific areas of need in the parish. Being able to paint a picture for those involved in discipleship of the ways in which God might be calling them to "go and make more disciples" can provide even more motivation for them to stay involved and remain committed to discipleship.

3. Meet people where they are at

In *Forming Intentional Disciples*[4], Sherry Weddell focuses on several thresholds of conversion that precede a person's choice to become an intentional disciple. Along with these thresholds, she describes a charism that is helpful for reaching someone at each threshold. I love her articulation of these charisms because it simplifies what we should be doing to help lead others towards intentional discipleship. Instead of just taking a general approach to ministry, it focuses our attention on the individual and what he or she needs. Do what you can to worry about nothing else except what each person needs.

4. Simply provide opportunities for people to connect

One of the important aspects of evangelization is connecting people in your parish to each other. Be sure to take time to do things that simply create community and help people involved in discipleship in your parish to connect to one another. When people involved in common mission begin to share and grow together it creates a movement that can be unstoppable...in a very good way.

5. Require evangelization as part of your small groups

Another helpful thing is to expect all of your discipleship groups to have intentionally committed to some sort of evangelization outreach in the parish or community. It should be expected that any discipleship in the parish be mission-oriented, meaning it doesn't exist just for the people involved. This can include so many different things, but allowing the groups to decide what they want to do can bring about some awesome ideas. This is pastoral formation and should be part of the life of a disciple, anyway.

6. Have Fun!

One of my greatest struggles is always thinking that we have to be doing something deeply formative. But one of the most attractive things you

---

[4] Sherry Weddell, *Forming Intentional Disciples*, (Huntington, Our Sunday Visitor Publishing, 2012), chapters 5-8.

can do that draws people into your parish ministry is to simply have fun! Have fun with your leaders, with your groups, and with your events. Do what you can to make the Church a parish family that is attractive and fun to be a part of. This alone will become a mode of evangelization that will shift the way people understand and approach the Church.

11.
Step 4 - Adapt to Growth and Needs
Eric Gallagher

"The Church which "goes forth" is a community of missionary disciples
who take the first step"
- Pope Francis (EG, 24)

I have never really been someone who knows much about gardening. I
remember when I was young and watching my father as he started the
garden in our yard. Not really knowing exactly what needed to be done,
he carved out a little spot and tried planting a few things. Ten years
later, that same garden had grown to be about 10 times the size it was at
the beginning. The garden was now organized, all the tasks involved
with planting and tending it were timed perfectly, and it probably
actually seemed like less work for my dad than it was when he first
started it. The greatest part for me as a kid what the bounty that came
from that garden. Not only did the garden get bigger and better, but it
provided a better and more plentiful harvest for the family to enjoy. This
fourth step we introduce now is doing exactly what my father had done
with his garden. After you have spent time learning the process, seeing
how it works, and finding success, you can begin to replicate it as well as
try some new things.

As your Discipleship Focused Youth Ministry begins to grow in a parish,
new challenges will come. You will find yourself tilling soil in
previously untapped areas of the parish, you will be bringing on more
and more help to manage all that is going on, and soon you may find

yourself simply managing others who are doing the work instead of doing it all yourself.

It is hard to describe exactly how you approach this step in the process as it is more of a response to what is going on than actually moving forward and doing things differently. Here is a list of things that I have found often arise that are cause for adaptation and change what needs to be done, as well as short recommendations on how you might respond.

1. Groups will grow and need to be split
The goal is to allow the groups to evolve naturally. We usually say groups should be no more than 4-6 youth and two adults. Once a group gets larger than that, it becomes difficult to offer the intimacy and customization needed to foster discipleship. Encourage the leaders and those in the groups to discern how the group can split to maintain these important components while also encouraging them to do things with both groups together. They can still enjoy community with one another at times when the different groups come together, but they should understand that this larger community is a fruit of the depth that is reached through discipleship, which is harder to accomplish in the context of the larger group.

2. New groups will need to be formed, especially as student's graduate
Especially in the beginning stages, new groups can seem a bit awkward. Do not be afraid to let groups sit at 2-3 youth members. Navigating through change can be difficult, but if you are willing to simply talk with those involved, a solution becomes pretty clear. Do not rush into easy solutions, but discern together the connections that make the most sense to accommodate good formation opportunities for each individual.

3. More leaders will need to be trained
One of the key roles of the parish coordinator is to continually seek out and invite adults to be involved in the youth discipleship initiative. We encourage offering an initial boot camp for any new leaders who are

interested and then having them join in the regular (typically monthly) training and formation from then on.

4. Leadership will need several levels of depth as you begin to work with 10-20 adults as opposed to 4-6.
We have seen some creative ideas for this. Some coordinators enjoy working with a small group of adults, and they then have those adults meet with other adults. Some coordinators have held 2-3 monthly training times instead of just one that breaks the adults into smaller groups. The goal is to always ensure your adults are being fed and encouraged in their discipleship role.

5. Facility use will become a demand
Having small groups demands a lot of space. This is a great need to have. As Jim mentioned earlier, many parishes have been physically designed to accommodate a large group ministry model and do not work well if many small groups want to meet at the same time. Strive to be creative and accommodating to small groups as they desire to meet. If your diocese allows small groups to meet in homes, this can be one solution to the problem of limited space.

6. People will begin to push the boundaries
Once groups learn that they really do have permission to think big, they will begin to ask for things that seem a little crazy. Always be sure to maintain oversight and obedience with the leaders of the groups. As long as leaders are looking to you for permission, it gives you the ability to keep things under control. Do not be afraid to say "no" to leaders simply because it is just too much for right now.

7. Programs will sprout from the ground up that require oversight and accountability
When groups are growing and thriving, they will often desire to start their own program in the parish in addition to their discipleship group. Traditionally, a program or event couldn't be done in the parish if it wasn't planned or organized by the DRE or youth minister. In a

discipleship model, this is a great way to allow groups to serve and step up to fill certain areas of need. For example, one group wanted to host a monthly dodgeball night in the school gym. It was an awesome opportunity to invite new youth to come and be at the parish. Learn to trust your leaders, give them responsibility, and let ministry happen. It can be difficult to trust your leaders sometimes, but it is this trust that will really deepen the efforts parish-wide.

8. Certain demographics will need special attention

You may find at times that certain groups or people will need special attention. This may require you to reach out in a special way to students in a certain school system who do not seem to be engaged at all. You may need to develop a ministry that reaches out specifically to the athletes in the parish. It may even be good to offer one-time or ongoing programs for those with special family or personal circumstances like divorce, depression, etc. Be aware that sometimes a discipleship group may not be able to provide enough help in these specific areas, and be ready and available to offer extra help as needed. Keep an eye out for adults in the parish who can become the parish expert in some of these areas or to potentially develop a short study or workshop that can be made available on demand for a group or as a parish activity open and available to all.

9. Certain components of the faith will need to be brought out

I have found that every parish has a personality. Just like an individual, a parish often lacks a focus in one or more different areas. It is important that the pastor and the coordinator have an eye for these types of things and strive to infuse them into the vision of the small groups. An example might be to require groups to focus on vocations or sexuality, to demand that certain topics be taught because they have been neglected for whatever reason.

10. The discipleship group may not work for everyone

Discipleship groups are very much the norm, but they are not for everyone. It is important to remember that the goal is not necessarily to build up as many small discipleship groups as you can, but to look out for every youth and to help each one to be formed as a disciple. There will likely be youth in any parish who already have much of what a discipleship group has to offer (like strong, faith-filled friendships or good formation from their family or another mentor). I have seen many youth who prefer one-on-one mentorship or maybe even intensive study in the faith to spending time in more of a fellowship setting. Some youth simply don't have time for a weekly discipleship group, and that may be ok. Strive to make the discipleship group the norm, but be attentive to the needs of everyone and do not assume that a discipleship group will be what meets the needs of each person.

As you can tell, all of these things are very good "problems" to have in a parish. The more you can get your small groups on autopilot, the more freedom you as a coordinator will have to respond to these different circumstances. Be attentive to the various needs that arise, and take responsibility for discerning the ways in which to meet them. Staying close to those discipleship leaders in your parish who are investing in others will help you clearly identify specific challenges and solutions, enabling you as the parish coordinator to support them as best you can.

12.
Step 5 - Feed the Nations
Eric Gallagher

"True devotion does us no harm whatsoever,
but instead perfects all things"
- St. Francis De Sales

Returning for a moment to the memories of my father's garden, I wouldn't be giving him enough credit unless I mentioned the large amounts of food that were given away to others. I can remember dozens of jars of salsa and spicy carrots (I don't even know what spicy carrots are) in our cupboards, and every time someone came to visit, they would leave with several jars to take home. I would wager a guess that in the first year of growing his garden, he probably didn't have any produce that he would have been proud to even show anyone else (sorry, Dad, if that's not true!). My point is that it takes time to grow something in a way that it can then be given away freely.

The last step of the Discipleship Focused Youth Ministry process is to take the fruit that is coming from your parish and extend it to the broader Church family. If you have followed the steps laid out here and have patiently waited for each phase of growth to unfold in your parish, you should have many opportunities available for youth wherever they are at. Ongoing training and formation of leaders should be in place, and most of the ministry really should be operating in a semi-autopilot state. Overall, things are at least structured in a way that the youth ministry should be doing ok.

What you will observe at this point is that the youth ministry program is beginning to bleed into other aspects of the parish and of the community. Imagine these things happening in your parish:

- The youth discipleship groups inspire adults to start their own discipleship groups.
- Parent ministry is in greater demand because parents are learning the value of discipleship, and they desire to disciple their children more and more.
- Other parishes in town begin to get frustrated because their youth are going to YOUR Church!
- Vocations are flourishing, and you now have to support seminarians and religious who have come from your parish.
- Your parish is taking groups of youth to visit solid Catholic universities and Newman Centers because they are now evaluating their college choice on how much it will help them grow in their faith rather than the size of the dorm room or how pretty the campus is.
- When there is a need in the community, people are calling your parish because of its history of helping others.
- You begin to host regional or city-wide events just because you can!

There are so many things that can be done when your parish has confidence in what it is doing and where it is going. It is time to be that parish, be that Church, and be those people who are influencing the town and the world in a positive way. I believe that this is possible, but I believe it will take time. I don't think that this sort of abundance is anything that we can produce ourselves as leaders in the parish, but it will come from the depths of knowing and following Jesus Christ and sharing Him with others.

13.
How is DFYM Different?
Eric Gallagher

"If you want to build a ship, don't drum up people to collect wood and don't assign them tasks and work, but rather teach them to long for the endless immensity of the sea."
- Antoine de Saint-Exupery

In networking with hundreds of people involved in youth ministry and having lots of conversations about Discipleship Focused Youth Ministry, it is clear that many of the concepts and ideas that we are presenting in this book are not really "new" to many people. In fact, as we speak about some of the results you may expect as you begin to implement a more Discipleship Focused approach to youth ministry, it may not seem like anything too unique at all. There are other ways to achieve some of the same results, and we don't claim to have the one and only magic pill to make it happen.

However, in all my conversations with people who work in and teach about youth ministry, I really believe that Discipleship Focused Youth Ministry presents some fundamental ideas that are very much a shift from the way things have traditionally been done. These are the major changes that I have seen parishes need to make in order to allow the freedom that Discipleship Focused Youth Ministry offers to really happen.

DFYM is NOT a "One Size Fits All" Programming
I truly believe the days of having one program in the parish or even one program for each grade or sex are over. While programs can be very good and are usually used in some form within Discipleship Focused Youth Ministry to facilitate growth or meet a real need, they cannot be the primary or only way of reaching the youth. Discipleship Focused Youth Ministry utilizes the process of discipleship and the skills of the individual leader to craft a customized plan of formation for each person, which can include anything from one-on-one counsel from an elder to being involved in a larger program or mission. It is flexible to meet the specific needs of each unique individual.

DFYM is a Ground-Up Approach
Developing a solution to certain challenges using a top-down structure in ministry - a solution that people believe will be the answer to their problems or will do everything for them - can be incredibly dangerous. I have seen this so often in youth ministry and religious education. It's part of the reason why parents drop their kids off in the parking lot, and it seems as though that is the extent of the effort they make to raise their children up in the faith.

When ministry is coming from the top-down, it means that the pastor or youth minister has decided that they want to establish or build something that they believe will solve a problem or address a need in the parish. It is their program. Discipleship Focused Youth Ministry encourages ministry to be done from the ground-up. It means that the things happening should be inspired by the parish or through its efforts, but that they do not necessarily belong to it. A discipleship group might begin as a fruit of a recent youth conference. The group should seek permission and oversight from the parish, but if at any time the group decides they no longer want to meet, the group would no longer exist. Requiring ministry to happen ground-up requires the right people to step up and become part of the solution. If they are being supported and formed by the parish, this type of response begins to become very real and naturally flow from growth in the Christian life.

It should be said that sometimes there literally may not be someone available and ready to start discipleship in a parish. In this case, it may require the help and resources of the parish, or it may just require some time, prayer, and investing in a few potential people. Remember that you can start with just one and let it slowly grow from there. Also, there really can be a great benefit to offering parish programs. I recommend that programs exist either to encourage and promote discipleship to happen naturally or to offer opportunities for those in discipleship to be part of a larger community.

Discipleship is Reaching Someone Through Someone
It wasn't just through the apostles, whom he had discipled for three years so that they might learn to live as he lived and do what he did, that Jesus used someone or something else to accomplish his work. He used mud to heal a blind man, he used the Blessed Mother to bring him into this world, he uses priests to bring us the Eucharist. The most effective way you can grow and sustain a ministry that exists even when you are gone (like Jesus did!) is to equip and empower others to do it. In short, a youth minister's job is not to minister to the youth, but to form those who should. In a Discipleship Focused Youth Ministry model, a youth minister acts more as a consultant and mentor to those who really do have the responsibility of forming our young people, which is the whole parish family and primarily the parents.

The Balance of True Freedom
I remember growing up playing with my grandmother's pendulum clock. I would grab the pendulum and stop it, and as I let go, it would slowly build up momentum until it was swinging in full motion again. This serves as a great analogy for something I have observed in youth ministry over the years. On one end of the continuum, I find parishes that simply allow the adults and youth to do whatever they want to do, and it becomes a very dangerous place. Or maybe they hire a young,

energetic youth minister and set them free with little or no oversight or accountability whatsoever. It might be nice to have the freedom to be with the youth, build friendships, and have no boundaries when it comes to helping them, but it would also be nice to have some guidance and parameters to at least know that you are doing what you should be doing and to keep you out of trouble. While it might seem like this person has all the freedom they need to be effective, without proper boundaries, they are not really free at all.

On the other end of the continuum, I have seen parishes that are so over-protective of the youth that it practically chokes the life out of any ministry that even had a chance to exist. They place 20 youth in four walls with two adults and just pray that nothing bad happens.

I don't think either of these are the right approach. Discipleship Focused Youth Ministry allows discipleship to happen while still having measures to ensure good oversight and accountability by appointing someone who will oversee the groups and relationships in the parish. As a small group leader in my own parish, I present what I am interested in doing in discipleship to the parish coordinator and the parents of the youth I desire to work with, they approve it, and off we go! Doing it this way, I experience the freedom to do what I think is best, but the parish's oversight grants me the freedom - in obedience - to know that what I am doing is what the pastor (or his delegate) would want me to be doing as well.

Results vs. Tasks
The last big shift I propose through Discipleship Focused Youth Ministry is that we would begin to foster good leaders and formation by evaluating ministry based on the results we are striving for and not the tasks that we are doing. If our mission is to form those who are forming others, we must begin to help them develop the skills to know and the abilities to implement the things they should be doing rather than just telling them what to do. I can tell someone they need to teach Chapters 10 and 11 in the course of a night, and they would likely do it. In this

case, they are likely not as concerned about the impact those chapters make on the youth to whom they are presenting to, they just feel the weight of the necessity of get through the chapters. They will tend to be more focused on the chapters than on the results those chapters are intended to produce.

If you can empower an adult to seek results that reflect a young person now knows and is following after Christ, they will understand the challenge and will discern the means to get that person there. They will begin to think like a youth minister and will no longer simply wait to do whatever the youth minister tells them to do. Like my dad learning to grow a garden, they will grow in knowing how to do youth ministry by looking at the results of their efforts in the past.

As I said before, you may be doing some of these things and thinking in these ways already, and that is great! But making every one of these shifts is necessary before a parish's efforts in discipleship will begin to be truly effective. They will require a little more trust (and maybe some letting go) on the part of the pastor and the youth minister, but they will finally grant the freedom and the partnership that I believe many in the Church desire and that the parents and parish community need.

14.
10 Things You Should Know or Do Before You Say Go!
Eric Gallagher

"Go therefore and make disciples of all nations, baptizing them in the name of the Father and of the Son and of the Holy Spirit, teaching them to observe all that I have commanded you; and lo, I am with you always, to the close of the age."
- Matthew 28:19-20

Whether or not you have had any sort of youth ministry in your parish before, moving towards a more Discipleship Focused Youth Ministry mindset will not be easy. After assisting numerous parishes with this vision and walking with them as they strive to forge new paths in the way the parish thinks about and does ministry, we have learned a few things from our experiences. Here are ten suggestions on things you should know or do before you set out on this journey.

Discipleship Is Messy
The hardest thing about discipleship is that from the outside, it's confusing. It can come across as exclusive, and it's difficult to promote by an open invitation to everyone because in the sense that it requires a commitment, it's not. It is open to anyone, but only to those who are ready to commit. This often leads to people misunderstanding what is actually going on, which then requires a lot of "cleanup" to clarify the vision and care for those who are anxious about what is happening.

Your Pastor MUST be on Board

Because discipleship is messy, it is vital that your pastor is on board with what you are doing. We have run into several situations where a parish started down the path of Discipleship Focused Youth Ministry and as things got a little messy, the pastor became anxious and things never really progressed from there. Be sure you communicate often with your pastor and share the good things the Lord is doing in your parish through discipleship.

Discipleship MUST be the priority

This is especially for those who already have certain programming in place in their parish. As you carve out a space and create margin in your schedule, make the time you spend with your discipleship leaders a priority. Investing in others and beginning a discipleship approach requires much attention. Like growing a garden, if you leave things unattended for too long and you do not give them proper care, they will die. As much as possible, allow your other commitments and programs to be in maintenance mode and delegate as much as possible so that you are able to truly invest in those beginning to learn the ropes of discipleship with you.

You Need to Learn to Trust

When I first wrote this suggestion, I thought, "I can't write that; there may be some people who have the ability to trust already." But I honestly believe that discipleship requires a deeper amount of faith and greater trust in those whom we send out into discipleship than has ever been required of us before. When you start to think that it would be better to just do things yourself, imagine our Lord as he sent out his apostles for the first time. Knowing that they would make mistakes was precisely the plan as his goal was not just to make more disciples, but to use his relationship with the apostles and the mission of discipleship to form them. Our Lord desires to form you and deepen your faith through your role in leading discipleship in your parish.

Transition Is Ok

Discipleship takes time and will require a lot of patience with yourself and with others. Do not be afraid to take a few years if needed to transition what you currently have to this discipleship focused approach. Learning to delegate and trust others to run parts of your other programs is a great way to build that muscle of trust that is required for discipleship anyway. If you don't have much going on right now, do not feel like you have jump right in and start discipleship groups right away. Sometimes, it can even be appropriate to shift the way current programs are done in order to plant seeds of interest in discipleship. Just because another parish is already doing many of the things we present in this book does not necessarily mean that you have to be there today.

Get Connected

Because Discipleship Focused Youth Ministry takes time and is not easily understood (even by us sometimes!), it is important to get connected to others who are desiring the same things and see ministry the same way as we do. God desires to form us through this journey as well and surround us with people who will continue to help us deepen our understanding of what God is doing.

Cling to Prayer

The single best way that you can learn to lead is by learning to follow. Be committed to daily prayer, learn to be less anxious about what you should be doing, and follow the Lord where He is desiring to take you. Become aware of the many ways in which the Lord is present to you throughout the day, and look to him as you encounter people each day, as you experience growth and change in your parish, and as you see people being changed over time.

The Right People Have Been Waiting for This

One of the biggest surprises I have had since diving into Discipleship Focused Youth Ministry is that those who are willing and able to get involved in discipleship are thriving. Those people who are disciples themselves know what it's like to be formed by God. They have fought through many of the struggles a disciple has in trusting and following Christ. Who better to instruct our youth on doing the same?

Please! Please! Please! Start Slow

Learning about the potential of discipleship can be extremely exciting. The reality is that this model is something that needs to be experienced and learned, which takes time. Remember that part of the process of building a discipleship focused ministry is actually leading and forming adults to do so. It could take several years before it begins to click with some adults. Be patient with them, and remain focused on the people involved and not so concerned about the number of youth you have in discipleship.

Remain Focused

Yes, there is a reason we call it Discipleship "Focused" Youth Ministry. Remaining focused on the basic elements needed to cultivate an atmosphere of discipleship in a parish is essential for working through the steps mentioned in this book. You will likely be surprised at the many opportunities for distraction that will come to you throughout this process, and it will be difficult for you to say no. Be intentional about everything that is changed, everything that is cut, and everything that is added to your plate as you begin this journey towards discipleship.

15.
Where to Go for More?
Eric Gallagher

*"Each of you has a special mission in life,
and you are each called to be a disciple of Christ."*
- Saint John Paul II

This book is really intended to paint a picture of what is possible and what we have been seeing in parishes that are beginning to make the shift towards a more discipleship focused approach to youth ministry.

I created DiscipleshipYM.com in order to provide a place where people like you can go in order to learn more about Discipleship Focused Youth Ministry and to have access to the many resources that are being developed and used by parishes that are striving to shift towards this approach.

Here are just a few things that are offered on the site:

Regular Blog Posts
Valuable insights and lessons learned from those involved in Discipleship Focused Youth Ministry. Many find this content alone good enough to generate dialogue and for use in offering training for discipleship leaders in their parish.

Reading List

The top recommended books, articles, and other print materials to help those desiring to grow as discipleship leaders.

Online Training and Formation

The same training that we provide to parishes around the country is now available online. We provide training for parish discipleship coordinators, diocesan directors, and small group leaders. We have developed a website devoted specifically to this training at DiscipleshipTraining.com.

Facebook Discussion Group

This is probably the best place to connect with others, ask questions, and engage with the Discipleship Focused Youth Ministry tribe. Look for a link on the site.

These are just a few of the ways in which DiscipleshipYM.com can be a resource for you. Look forward to more coming soon, and know that we are here to help in any way that we are able. Do not hesitate to connect with us through the site or through any sort of social networking.

Our prayer is that all parishes throughout the world would be open to receiving all that the Lord desires to do through the graces that come in responding to the call of the New Evangelization. This book and the efforts through DiscipleshipYM.com are a simple effort to share what we are experiencing in that call. We invite others to walk the journey with us as we continue to grow in our understanding of what it means to be a disciple of Jesus Christ and to respond to the call to "go and make more disciples".

Made in the USA
Middletown, DE
13 August 2017